Thank You

FOR BEING MY
Mother

Thank You

FOR BEING MY

Mother

Copyright ©2003 Elm Hill Books, an imprint of J. Countryman®, a division of Thomas Nelson, Inc.
Nashville, TN 37214

All rights reserved. No part of this book may be reproduced, stored in a retrieval system, or transmitted in any form or by any means—electronic, mechanical, photocopying, recording, or any other—except for brief quotations in printed reviews, without prior written permission of the publisher.

The quoted ideas expressed in this book (but not scripture verses) are not, in all cases, exact quotations, as some have been edited for clarity and brevity. In all cases, the author has attempted to maintain the speaker's original intent. In some cases, quoted material for this book was obtained from secondary sources, primarily print media. While every effort was made to ensure the accuracy of these sources, the accuracy cannot be guaranteed. For additions, deletions, corrections, or clarifications in future editions of this text, please contact Paul Shepherd, Executive Director for Elm Hill Books.
Email pshepherd@elmhillbooks.com.

Scripture quotations are taken from:

The Holy Bible, New King James Version (NKJV) Copyright © 1982 by Thomas Nelson, Inc. Used by permission.

New Century Version (NCV) © 1987, 1988, 1991 by Word Publishing, a division of Thomas Nelson, Inc. All rights reserved. Used by permission.

Cover Design by Denise Rosser
Page Layout by Bart Dawson

ISBN 1-4041-8455-4

Printed in the United States of America

To My Mother

CONTENTS

Introduction	11
1. Thank You for . . . Being My Mother	13
2. Thank You for . . . Your Love	21
3. Thank You for . . . The Memories	37
4. Thank You for . . . Your Care and Kindness	45
5. Thank You for . . . Your Encouragement	57
6. Thank You for . . . Listening and Understanding	67
7. Thank You for . . . Your Patience	77
8. Thank You for . . . Laughing with Me	85
9. Thank You for . . . Sharing My Dreams	95
10. Thank You for . . . Your Prayers	105
11. Thank You for . . . The Lessons	115
12. Thank You for . . . Your Sacrifices	125
13. Thank You for . . . Your Example	137
14. A Mother Is . . .	151

INTRODUCTION

Motherhood, other claims to the contrary, is the world's oldest profession—and its most important. This little book celebrates the joys and responsibilities of the job.

Lin Yutang observed, "Of all the rights of women, the greatest is to be a mother." Yutang understood a good mother does more than give birth; she shapes life.

The Bible verses and quotations on these pages remind us a mother, as she raises her child, places her mark upon eternity. And we children are eternally grateful.

Thanks, Mom . . . for everything!

Thank You for...
BEING MY MOTHER

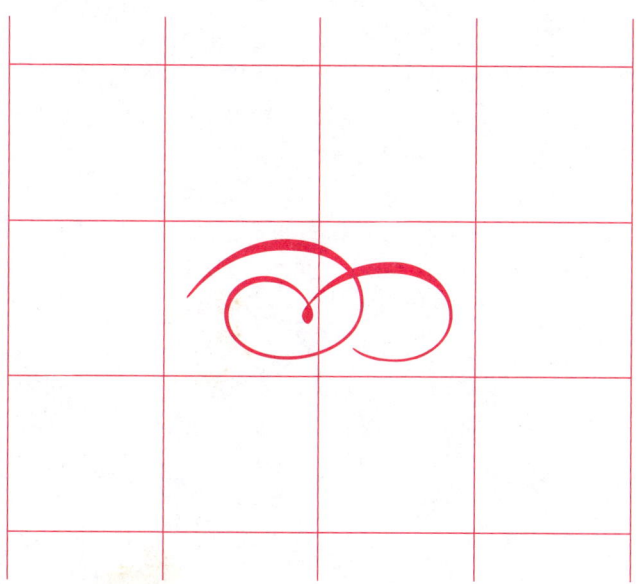

Her children rise up and call her blessed.

PROVERBS 31:28 NKJV

THANK YOU FOR BEING MY MOTHER

DEAR MOM,

Thank you for being my mother. Thanks for the love, the care, the work, the discipline, the wisdom, the support, and the faith. Thanks for being a concerned parent and a worthy example. Thanks for giving life and teaching it. Thanks for being patient with me, even when you were tired, or frustrated—or both. Thanks for changing diapers and wiping away tears. Thanks for being a woman who is worthy of both admiration and love.

You deserve my thanks, Mom, but you deserve so much more. You deserve our family's undying gratitude. You deserve happiness, contentment, and peace. May you enjoy God's blessings always. May you never, ever forget how much we love you.

Signed,
Your Loving Child

THANK YOU FOR... BEING MY MOTHER

> THE WOMAN WHO CREATES AND SUSTAINS A HOME IS A CREATOR SECOND ONLY TO GOD.
>
> HELEN HUNT JACKSON

GOD COULD NOT BE
EVERYWHERE,
SO HE MADE MOTHERS.

JEWISH PROVERB

> THANK YOU FOR . . . BEING MY MOTHER

Mother is the name for God on the lips
and in the hearts of little children.

WILLIAM MAKEPEACE THACKERY

Mothers must model the tenderness we need.
Our world can't find it anywhere else.

CHARLES SWINDOLL

Most of all the other beautiful things in life
come by twos and threes, by dozens
and hundreds. Plenty of roses, stars,
sunsets, rainbows, brothers, and sisters,
aunts and cousins, but only
one Mother in the whole world.

KATE DOUGLAS WIGGIN

Parents: persons who spend half their time
worrying how a child will turn out,
and the rest of the time wondering
when a child will turn in.

TED COOK

A parent acquires all rights
of the most sacred friendship.

MARY WOLLSTONECRAFT SHELLEY

From good parents come a good child.

ARISTOTLE

THANK YOU FOR . . . BEING MY MOTHER

THERE IS NO FRIENDSHIP,
NO LOVE, LIKE THAT
OF THE MOTHER
FOR THE CHILD.

HENRY WARD BEECHER

THANK YOU FOR BEING MY MOTHER

A MOTHER IS...
THE HOLIEST THING ALIVE.

SAMUEL TAYLOR COLERIDGE

Thank You for...
YOUR LOVE

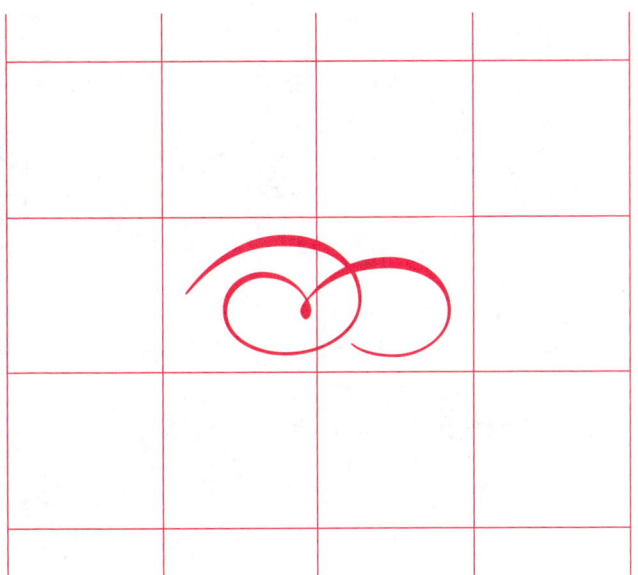

And now abide faith, hope, love, these three;
but the greatest of these is love.

1 CORINTHIANS 13:13 NKJV

DEAR MOM,

The first lesson a caring mother teaches her child is the lesson of love—and you taught it well.

A mother's love is like no other: a gift that is freely given, demonstrated by deed and word, begins before birth, and endures forever.

Great moms come in a wide range of shapes, sizes, colors, temperaments and nationalities; but they all share a singular trait: maternal love. Sometimes, that devotion is tested to the limits. Even well-intended children occasionally behave in ways only a mother could love. Thankfully, you've forgiven my shortcomings, and for that, I'm grateful. Your heart is big enough to love me in spite my imperfections . . . thank goodness—and Thank You!

THANK YOU FOR . . . YOUR LOVE

A MOTHER'S LOVE!
O HOLY,
BOUNDLESS THING!
FOUNTAIN WHOSE
WATERS NEVER
CEASE TO SPRING.

MARGUERITE BLESSINGTON

MATERNAL LOVE:
A MIRACULOUS
SUBSTANCE WHICH
GOD MULTIPLIES
AS HE DIVIDES IT.

VICTOR HUGO

THANK YOU FOR . . . YOUR LOVE

No human creature could receive or contain
so vast a flood of love as I often felt
after the birth of my child.

DOROTHY DAY

Love is a great beautifier.

LOUISA MAY ALCOTT

A mother's love is like a circle;
it has no beginning and no ending.
It keeps going around and around,
always expanding, touching everyone
who comes in contact with it.

ART URBAN

No language can express the power
and beauty and heroism of a mother's love.

EDWIN CHAPIN

The story of a love is not important—
what is important is that one is capable of love.
It is perhaps the only glimpse
we are permitted of eternity.

HELEN HAYES

The ability to love is the heart of the matter.
That is how we must measure our success
or failure at being parents.

GLORIA VANDERBILT

THANK YOU FOR . . . YOUR LOVE

YOU DON'T HAVE TO DESERVE YOUR MOTHER'S LOVE.

ROBERT FROST

THANK YOU FOR BEING MY MOTHER

A WOMAN WHO IS LOVED
ALWAYS HAS SUCCESS.

VICKI BAUM

The best and most beautiful things
in the world cannot be seen or even touched.
They must be felt with the heart.

HELEN KELLER

Accustom yourself continually to make
many acts of love, for they enkindle
and melt the soul.

ST. TERESA OF AVILA

Love is not a state, it is a direction.

SIMONE WEIL

> Love is a multiplication.
> MARJORY STONEMAN DOUGLAS

> Whoever loves true life, will love true love.
> ELIZABETH BARRETT BROWNING

> Nobody has ever measured, not even poets, how much the heart can hold.
> ZELDA FITZGERALD

*BELOVED,
IF GOD SO LOVED US,
WE ALSO OUGHT TO LOVE
ONE ANOTHER.*

1 JOHN 4:11 NKJV

THANK YOU FOR BEING MY MOTHER

MOTHER'S LOVE GROWS BY GIVING.

CHARLES LAMB

THANK YOU FOR . . . YOUR LOVE

Love doesn't just sit there, like stone;
it has to be made, like bread,
remade all the time, made new.

URSULA K. LE GUIN

Love will not always linger longest
with those who hold it in too clenched a fist.

ALICE DUER MILLER

Until I truly loved, I was alone.

CAROLINE NORTON

THANK YOU FOR BEING MY MOTHER

THE GIVING OF LOVE IS AN EDUCATION IN ITSELF.

ELEANOR ROOSEVELT

> THANK YOU FOR . . . YOUR LOVE

TO LOVE IS TO RECEIVE
A GLIMPSE OF HEAVEN.

KAREN SUNDE

> YOU HAVE TO LOVE
> YOUR CHILDREN
> UNSELFISHLY.
> THAT'S HARD.
> BUT IT'S THE ONLY WAY.
>
> — BARBARA BUSH

Thank You for...
THE MEMORIES

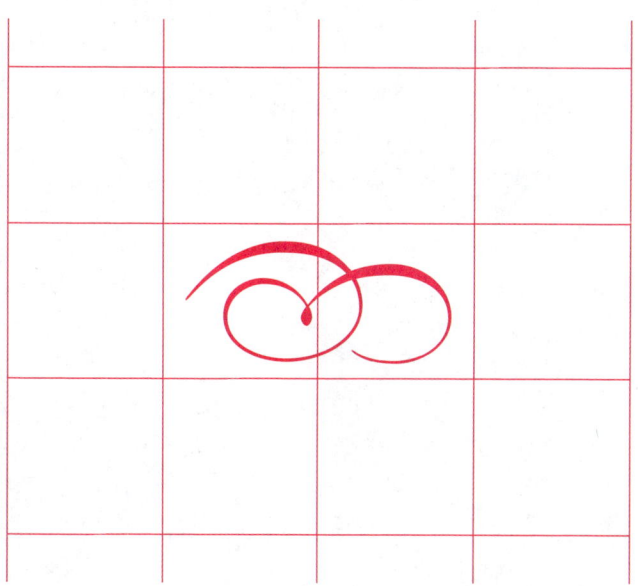

I thank my God upon every remembrance of you.

PHILIPPIANS 1:3 NKJV

DEAR MOM,

Thanks for the memories. Happy memories are always precious, but memories of you and our family are among the most precious of all.

Even when you and I are separated by distance and time, we are never really apart: we always have each other in our thoughts, our hearts, and our prayers.

You have given me so much. I think about your gifts more than you might imagine. The memories we share are a joy and comfort to me—I pray you feel the same way. You deserve the best of everything, including the very best memories of our times together.

THANK YOU FOR . . . THE MEMORIES

NOTHING IS AS PRECIOUS AS MY MEMORIES OF MY MOMMA.

DOLLY PARTON

> THANK YOU FOR BEING MY MOTHER

GOD GAVE US MEMORIES THAT WE MIGHT HAVE ROSES IN DECEMBER.

JAMES BARRIE

THANK YOU FOR . . . THE MEMORIES

> To be able to enjoy one's past
> is to be able to live twice.
>
> MARTIAL

> Remembered joys are never past.
>
> JAMES MONTGOMERY

> Cherish all your happy moments.
> They make a fine cushion for old age.
>
> BOOTH TARKINGTON

THANK YOU FOR BEING MY MOTHER

THE BEST THINGS
YOU CAN GIVE
YOUR CHILDREN,
NEXT TO GOOD HABITS,
ARE GOOD MEMORIES.

SYDNEY J. HARRIS

THANK YOU FOR . . . THE MEMORIES

To be in your children's memories tomorrow,
you have to be in their lives today.

ANONYMOUS

We must always have old memories
and young hopes.

ARSENE HOUSSAYE

I believe the true function of age is memory.
I'm recording as fast as I can.

RITA MAY BROWN

THANK YOU FOR BEING MY MOTHER

WHEN CHILDREN BECOME
ADULTS, THEY REMEMBER
THE LITTLE THINGS
YOU DID TOGETHER,
LIKE PLAYING BALL,
ROASTING MARSHMALLOWS,
OR HIKING A TRAIL.
THEY RARELY
REMEMBER TOYS.

BARBARA JOHNSON

Thank You for...
YOUR CARE AND KINDNESS

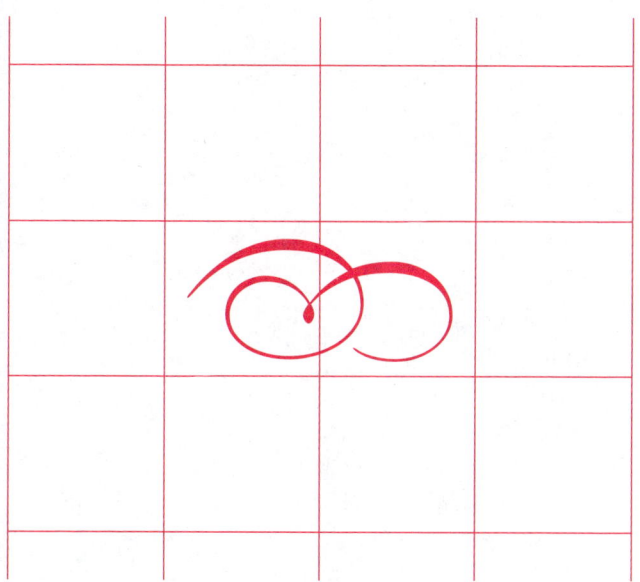

*And may the Lord make you increase
and abound in love to one another and to all.*

1 THESSALONIANS 3:12 NKJV

DEAR MOM,

Thanks for your care, concern, help, and kindness. Even in your busiest moments, you made time for me. Through your words and deeds, you have taught me a lesson that will last a lifetime: the power of compassion.

As a mother, you have always understood the importance of a kind word and the value of a helping hand. As your child, I am the beneficiary of your generous spirit. I will forever be grateful.

THANK YOU FOR . . . YOUR CARE AND KINDNESS

A MOTHER'S ARMS
ARE MADE OF
TENDERNESS.

VICTOR HUGO

THANK YOU FOR BEING MY MOTHER

More than any other human relationship,
overwhelmingly more, motherhood means being
instantly interruptible, responsive, responsible.

TILLIE OLSEN

My mother has not only always been able
to do everything, she's often done
everything at the same time.

COKIE ROBERTS

Mama was like a flowing river,
blessing the banks of life around her.

MARGARET JENSEN

THANK YOU FOR . . . YOUR CARE AND KINDNESS

OUR CHILDREN ARE
OUR MOST IMPORTANT
GUESTS: THEY ENTER
OUR HOME, ASK FOR
CAREFUL ATTENTION,
STAY AWHILE, AND THEN
LEAVE TO FOLLOW
THEIR OWN WAY.

HENRI NOUWEN

> If you stop to be kind,
> you must swerve often from your path.
>
> MARY WEBB

> No act of kindness, no matter how small,
> is ever wasted.
>
> AESOP

> The purpose of human life is to serve
> and to show compassion
> and the will to help others.
>
> ALBERT SCHWEITZER

THANK YOU FOR . . . YOUR CARE AND KINDNESS

Life is an exciting business and most exciting
when lived for other people.

HELEN KELLER

Kind words can be short and easy to speak,
but their echoes are truly endless.

MOTHER TERESA

Always try to be a little kinder than necessary.

J. M. BARRIE

Compassion abolishes the distance
between human beings.

HANNAH ARENDT

Kindness is the language which
the deaf can hear and the blind can see.

MARK TWAIN

Life is short and we never have enough time
for the hearts of those who travel
the way with us. O, be swift to love!
Make haste to be kind.

HENRI FRÉDÉRIC AMIEL

THANK YOU FOR . . . YOUR CARE AND KINDNESS

You will accomplish more by kind words
and a courteous manner than by anger
and sharp rebuke, which should never be used,
except in necessity.

ST. ANGELA MERICI

You give little when you give your possessions.
It is when you give of yourself
that you truly give.

KHALIL GIBRAN

OUR LIVES, WE ARE TOLD,
ARE BUT FLEETING
AT BEST, LIKE ROSES
THEY FADE AND DECAY;
THEN LET US DO GOOD
WHILE THE PRESENT
IS OURS, BE USEFUL
AS LONG AS WE STAY.

Fanny Crosby

> THANK YOU FOR . . . YOUR CARE AND KINDNESS

There is no love which does not become help.

PAUL TILLICH

Too often we underestimate the power
of a touch, a smile, a kind word, a listening ear,
an honest compliment, or the smallest act
of caring, all of which have the potential
to turn a life around.

LEO BUSCAGLIA

*And be kind to one another, tenderhearted,
forgiving one another, just as God
in Christ forgave you.*

EPHESIANS 4:32 NKJV

THANK YOU FOR BEING MY MOTHER

> MOST THINGS HAVE
> AN ESCAPE CLAUSE,
> BUT CHILDREN
> ARE FOREVER.
>
> LEWIS GRIZZARD

Thank You for...
YOUR ENCOURAGEMENT

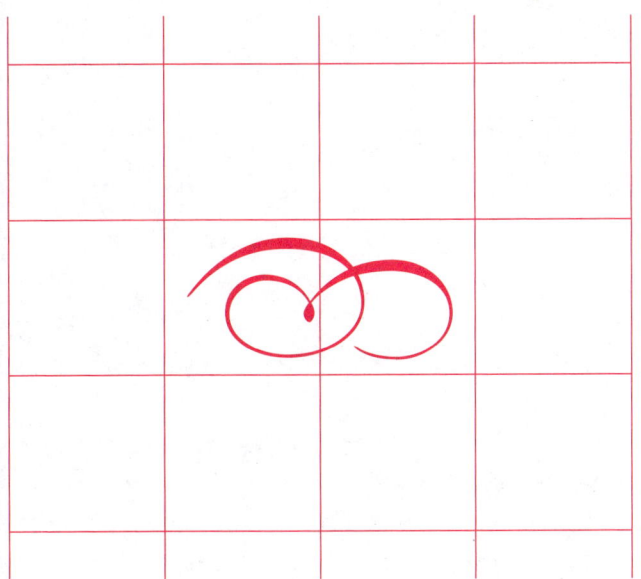

A word fitly spoken is like apples of gold in settings of silver.

PROVERBS 25:11 NKJV

THANK YOU FOR BEING MY MOTHER

DEAR MOM,

Thanks for your encouragement. Even when I did not believed in myself, you believed in me . . . and it showed.

A mother's attitude is contagious. If she is optimistic and upbeat, the family will tend to be likewise. But if a mother falls prey to pessimism and doubt, the family suffers right along with her.

Thankfully, you never gave up on me. You never stopped believing in my abilities. Eventually, because of you, I believe in myself. And that, Mom, is the power of encouragement.

THANK YOU FOR . . . YOUR ENCOURAGEMENT

MY MOTHER TOLD ME
I WAS BLESSED,
AND I HAVE ALWAYS
TAKEN HER WORD FOR IT.

DUKE ELLINGTON

THANK YOU FOR BEING MY MOTHER

> I'M NOT JUST YOUR MOTHER. I'M ALSO YOUR BIGGEST FAN.
>
> VIRGINIA CRISWELL

THANK YOU FOR . . . YOUR ENCOURAGEMENT

A really great person is the person
who makes every person feel great.

G. K. CHESTERTON

Words are more powerful than perhaps
anyone suspects, and once deeply ingrained
in a child's mind, they are not easily eradicated.

MAY SARTON

The greatest good you can do for another
is not just to share your riches,
but to reveal to him his own.

BENJAMIN DISRAELI

Never cease to be convinced that life
might be better . . . your own and others.

ANDRÉ GIDE

For every one of us who succeeds,
it's because there's somebody there
to show us the way.

OPRAH WINFREY

Correction does much, but encouragement
does more. Encouragement after censure
is as the sun after a shower.

GOETHE

THANK YOU FOR . . . YOUR ENCOURAGEMENT

KEEP YOUR FEARS
TO YOURSELF,
BUT SHARE
YOUR COURAGE
WITH OTHERS.

ROBERT LOUIS STEVENSON

THANK YOU FOR BEING MY MOTHER

IF YOU THINK YOU CAN,
YOU CAN.
AND IF YOU THINK
YOU CAN'T,
YOU'RE RIGHT.

Mary Kay Ash

THANK YOU FOR . . . YOUR ENCOURAGEMENT

Optimism is that faith that leads
to achievement. Nothing can be done
without hope and confidence.

HELEN KELLER

One of the things I learned the hard way
was that it doesn't pay to get discouraged.
Keeping busy and making optimism
a way of life can restore
your faith in yourself.

LUCILLE BALL

THANK YOU FOR BEING MY MOTHER

WHEN SOMEONE DOES
SOMETHING GOOD,
APPLAUD!
YOU'LL MAKE
TWO PEOPLE
FEEL GOOD.

SAM GOLDWYN

Thank You for...
LISTENING AND UNDERSTANDING

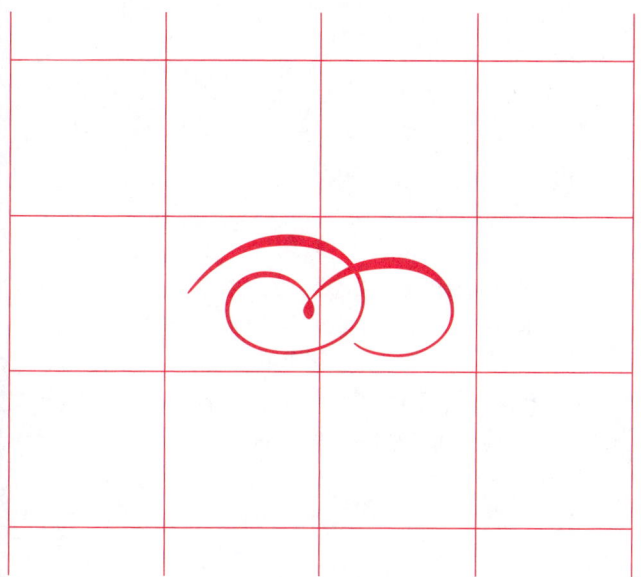

Wise people can also listen . . . .
PROVERBS 1:5 NCV

DEAR MOM,

Thanks for listening . . . and for understanding. Sometimes I'm quite sure you must have been frustrated by the things I said and did. But you listened anyway. Sometimes you understood me far better than I understood myself.

Of course you were willing to share your advice (which, I regret to admit, I sometimes ignored.) But you were also willing to let me make my own mistakes. Even when I faltered or failed, you never stopped loving me. And I never stopped loving you.

THANKYOU FOR... LISTENING AND UNDERSTANDING

THE MORE A CHILD
BECOMES AWARE OF
A PARENT'S WILLINGNESS
TO LISTEN, THE MORE
A PARENT WILL BEGIN
TO HEAR.

GEORGE MACDONALD

THANK YOU FOR BEING MY MOTHER

I think the one lesson I have learned is
that there is no substitute
for paying attention.

DIANE SAWYER

Oh, I listen a lot and talk less.
You can't learn anything
when you're talking.

BING CROSBY

Listen with sincerity.

JOE GIRARD

THANKYOU FOR . . . LISTENING AND UNDERSTANDING

THE ART OF CONVERSATION LIES IN LISTENING.

MALCOLM FORBES

THANK YOU FOR BEING MY MOTHER

BE A GOOD LISTENER.
YOUR EARS WILL NEVER
GET YOU IN TROUBLE.

FRANK TYGER

THANK YOU FOR... LISTENING AND UNDERSTANDING

I grew up knowing I was accepted and loved,
and that made an incredible difference.

BERNIE SEIGEL

When you speak, ask questions.
Don't lecture.

DENIS WAITLEY

THANK YOU FOR BEING MY MOTHER

THE REASON THAT WE HAVE TWO EARS AND ONLY ONE MOUTH IS THAT WE MAY LISTEN THE MORE AND TALK THE LESS.

ZENO OF CITIUM

THANKYOU FOR . . . LISTENING AND UNDERSTANDING

Before I got married, I had six theories
about bringing up children;
now I have six children and no theories.

LORD ROCHESTER

The real art of conversation is not only
to say the right thing at the right place
but to leave unsaid the wrong thing
at the tempting moment.

DOROTHY NEVILL

The things that we feel most deeply we ought
to learn to be silent about, at least until
we have talked them over thoroughly with God.

ELISABETH ELLIOT

THANK YOU FOR BEING MY MOTHER

A MOTHER UNDERSTANDS WHAT HER CHILD DOESN'T SAY.

YIDDISH PROVERB

Thank You for...
YOUR PATIENCE

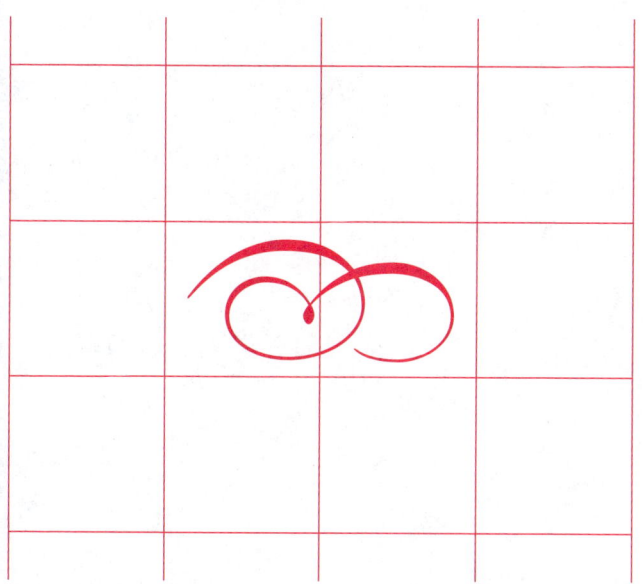

Be gentle to all, able to teach, patient.

2 TIMOTHY 2:24 NKJV

THANK YOU FOR BEING MY MOTHER

DEAR MOM,

Thanks for your patience. The rigors of motherhood can test the patience of the most even-tempered moms, and you were more patient than most.

All of us, parents and children alike, make our share of mistakes. When I made mine, you dried my tears, forgave me, and convinced me I could recover. As a grateful child, I thank God for your patience, your faith, and your love.

THANK YOU FOR . . . YOUR PATIENCE

A MOTHER'S PATIENCE
IS LIKE A TUBE
OF TOOTHPASTE:
IT'S NEVER QUITE GONE.

ANONYMOUS

THANK YOU FOR BEING MY MOTHER

Patience is the companion of wisdom.

ST. AUGUSTINE

Genius is nothing more than
a greater aptitude for patience.

BEN FRANKLIN

Patience achieves more than force.

EDMUND BURKE

THANK YOU FOR . . . YOUR PATIENCE

The key to everything is patience.
You get the chicken by hatching the egg,
not by smashing it.

ELLEN GLASGOW

Patience is bitter, but its fruit sweet.

JEAN-JACQUES ROUSSEAU

Teach us, O Lord, the disciplines of patience,
for to wait is often harder than to work.

PETER MARSHALL

> Sometimes in life the best
> and hardest thing to do is nothing.
>
> J. R. FREEMAN

> Adopt the pace of nature; her secret is patience.
>
> RALPH WALDO EMERSON

> Learn to accept in silence minor aggravations.
>
> WILLIAM OSLER

THANK YOU FOR . . . YOUR PATIENCE

Patience and diligence, like faith,
move mountains.

WILLIAM PENN

Have patience with all things, but mostly
with yourself. Don't lose courage considering
your own imperfections, but instantly
begin remedying them.
Every day begin the task anew.

ST. FRANCIS DE SALES

Endurance is nobler than strength,
and patience nobler than beauty.

JOHN RUSKIN

THANK YOU FOR BEING MY MOTHER

WHEN MY KIDS BECOME WILD AND UNRULY, I USE A NICE, SAFE PLAYPEN. WHEN THEY'RE FINISHED, I CLIMB OUT.

ERMA BOMBECK

Thank You for . . .
LAUGHING WITH ME

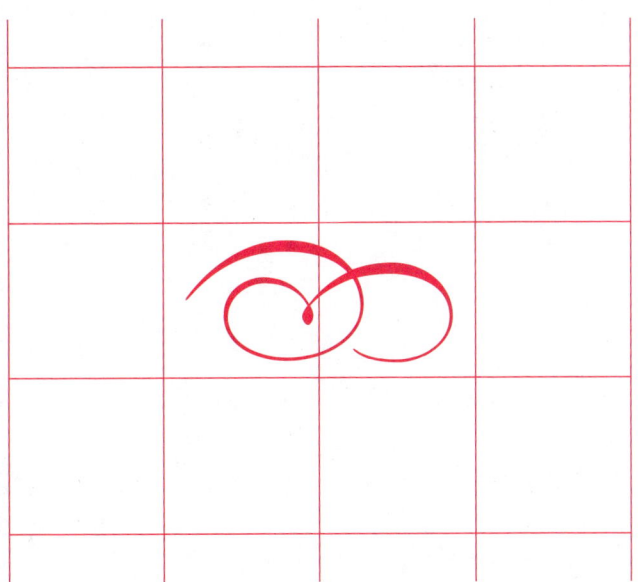

A merry heart makes a cheerful countenance....
PROVERBS 15:13 NKJV

THANK YOU FOR BEING MY MOTHER

DEAR MOM,

Thanks for the laughter. Laughter is medicine for the soul, but sometimes, amid the stresses of the day, we forget to take our medicine—you helped me remember to take mine.

When I'm tempted to take life a little too seriously, I think back on the good times we've shared, and I smile. Thank you for happy memories that give me comfort and joy—I pray those same memories will do the same for you.

THANK YOU FOR . . . LAUGHING WITH ME

MIRTH IS GOD'S MEDICINE.
EVERYBODY OUGHT
TO BATHE IN IT.

HENRY WARD BEECHER

THANK YOU FOR BEING MY MOTHER

Family jokes, though rightly cursed by strangers,
are the bond that keeps most families alive.

STELLA BENSON

There is nothing that rejuvenates the parched,
delicate spirits of children faster than
when a lighthearted spirit pervades
the home and laughter fills its halls.

JAMES DOBSON

A keen sense of humor helps us to overlook the
unbecoming, understand the unconventional,
tolerate the unpleasant, overcome
the unexpected, and outlast the unbearable.

BILLY GRAHAM

> LAUGHTER IS,
> BY DEFINITION,
> HEALTHY.
>
> DORIS LESSING

THANK YOU FOR BEING MY MOTHER

Laughter dulls the sharpest pain
and flattens out the greatest stress.
To share it is to give a gift of health.

BARBARA JOHNSON

Never miss a chance to laugh out loud.

DOUGLAS FAIRBANKS, JR.

The day returns and brings us the petty rounds
of irritating concerns and duties.
May we perform those duties
with laughter and kind faces.

ROBERT LOUIS STEVENSON

THANK YOU FOR . . . LAUGHING WITH ME

If I were given the opportunity to present a gift to the next generation, it would be the ability for each individual to learn to laugh at himself.

CHARLES SCHULZ

Most of all, learn to laugh at yourself; meet each day with a sense of humor.

WILFERD PETERSON

Wisdom lies in taking everything with good humor and a grain of salt.

GEORGE SANTAYANA

THANK YOU FOR BEING MY MOTHER

Learn laughter from little children by thinking
their thoughts, dreaming their dreams
and playing their games.

WILFERD PETERSON

Laugh and grow strong.

IGNATIUS LOYOLA

It is often just as sacred to laugh as it is to pray.

CHARLES SWINDOLL

THANK YOU FOR . . . LAUGHING WITH ME

Humor makes all things possible.
HENRY WARD BEECHER

Laugh and the world laughs with you.
Weep and you weep alone.
ELLA WHEELER WILCOX

Laughter is the shortest distance
between two people.
VICTOR BORGE

THANK YOU FOR BEING MY MOTHER

LAUGHTER IS AN INSTANT VACATION!

MILTON BERLE

Thank You for...
SHARING MY DREAMS

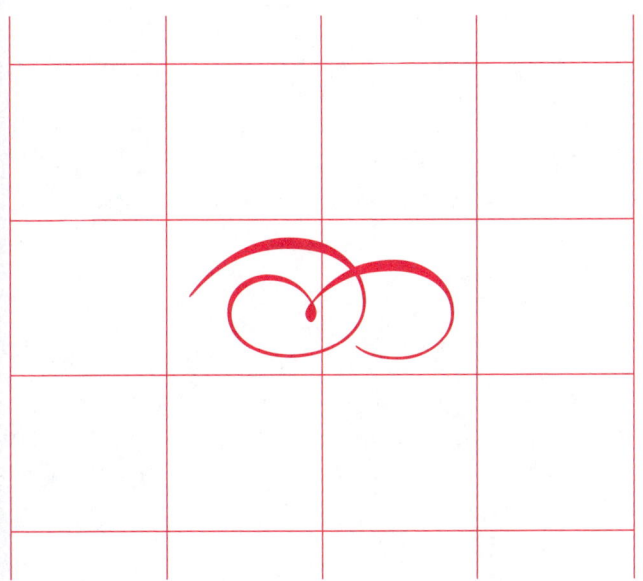

Be of good courage, and He shall strengthen your heart, all you who hope in the Lord.

PSALM 31:24 NKJV

THANK YOU FOR BEING MY MOTHER

DEAR MOM,

Thanks for sharing my dreams. When I summoned the courage to confide in you, you supported me, encouraged me, and trusted me. If you harbored any doubts, you hid them.

You should know that your faith in me is both exciting and contagious: I have finally caught it. Your hopes have become my hopes. As I work to make my dreams a reality, I know you and I are dreaming together.

THANK YOU FOR . . . SHARING MY DREAMS

A MOTHER'S LOVE SEES NO IMPOSSIBILITIES.

OLD SAYING

THANK YOU FOR BEING MY MOTHER

There are two lasting bequests we can hope
to give our children. One of these is roots;
the other, wings.

HODDING CARTER

Mother love is the fuel that enables
a normal human being to do the impossible.

MARION GARETTY

As a mother, my job is to take care of
the possible and trust God
with the impossible.

RUTH BELL GRAHAM

THANK YOU FOR... SHARING MY DREAMS

Too many people put their dreams "on hold."
It takes an uncommon amount of guts to put
your dreams on the line, to hold them up
and say, "How good or bad am I?"
That's where the courage comes in.

ERMA BOMBECK

Dreams do come true, if we only wish hard
enough. You can have anything in life if you
will sacrifice everything else for it.
"What will you have?" says God?
"Pay for it and take it."

JAMES BARRIE

Nothing happens unless first a dream.

CARL SANDBURG

Our dreams are who we are.
BARBARA SHER

Dreams are great. When they disappear
you may still be here,
but you will have ceased to live.
NANCY ASTOR

You're either a dream maker or a dream breaker.
MARK VICTOR HANSEN

THANK YOU FOR ... SHARING MY DREAMS

It is never too late to dream
or to start something new.
LUCI SWINDOLL

You don't always reach a dream in the way
you first see it. When you get there,
it's a different dream, but it's still a dream.
TINA TURNER

The future belongs to those who believe
in the beauty of their dreams.
ELEANOR ROOSEVELT

THANK YOU FOR BEING MY MOTHER

I avoid looking forward or backward,
and try to keep looking upward.

CHARLOTTE BRONTË

Everything that is done in the world
is done by hope.

MARTIN LUTHER

If you can dream it, you can do it.

WALT DISNEY

THANK YOU FOR . . . SHARING MY DREAMS

I CAN DO ALL THINGS THROUGH CHRIST WHO STRENGTHENS ME.

PHILIPPIANS 4:13 NKJV

THANK YOU FOR BEING MY MOTHER

MAMA EXHORTED HER CHILDREN AT EVERY OPPORTUNITY TO "JUMP AT DE SUN." WE MIGHT NOT LAND ON THE SUN, BUT AT LEAST WE WOULD GET OFF THE GROUND.

ZORA NEALE HURSTON

Thank You for...
YOUR PRAYERS

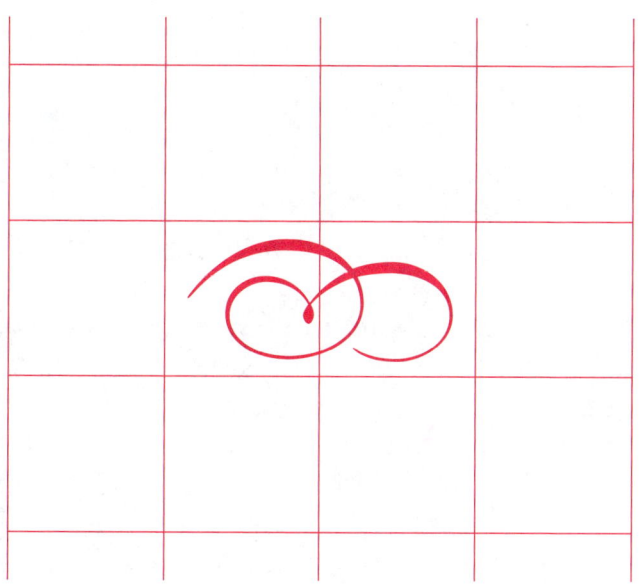

Rejoice always, pray without ceasing, in everything give thanks; for this is the will of God in Christ Jesus for you.

1 THESSALONIANS 5:16-18 NKJV

THANK YOU FOR BEING MY MOTHER

DEAR MOM,

Thank you for your prayers. God most certainly hears those prayers, and I am most certainly blessed by them.

Prayer changes things, and it changes us. As a mother whose heart is turned toward God, you know our Heavenly Father is always listening, and that He wants to hear from us right now. Thank you for the words you have spoken to Him on my behalf. Rest assured I, too, have quiet conversations with our Creator. Rest assured I'm praying for you, as you are praying for me.

THANK YOU FOR . . . YOUR PRAYERS

I REMEMBER MY MOTHER'S PRAYERS . . . AND THEY HAVE CLUNG TO ME ALL MY LIFE.

ABRAHAM LINCOLN

THANK YOU FOR BEING MY MOTHER

PRAYING FOR OUR CHILDREN
IS A NOBLE TASK.
THERE IS NOTHING MORE
SPECIAL, MORE PRECIOUS,
THAN TIME THAT A PARENT
SPENDS STRUGGLING
AND PONDERING WITH GOD
ON BEHALF OF A CHILD.

MAX LUCADO

THANK YOU FOR... YOUR PRAYERS

Pray, and let God worry.

MARTIN LUTHER

We must leave it to God to answer our prayers in His own wisest way. Sometimes, we are so impatient and think that God does not answer. God always answers! He never fails! Be still. Abide in Him.

MRS. CHARLES E. COWMAN

When there is a matter that requires definite prayer, pray until you believe God and until you can thank Him for His answer.

HANNAH WHITALL SMITH

Any concern that is too small to be turned
into a prayer is too small
to be made into a burden.

CORRIE TEN BOOM

Prayer guards hearts and minds
and causes God to bring peace out of chaos.

BETH MOORE

Is prayer your steering wheel or your spare tire?

CORRIE TEN BOOM

THANK YOU FOR . . . YOUR PRAYERS

Prayer is a long rope with a strong hold.
HARRIET BEECHER STOWE

As we join together in prayer, we draw on
God's enabling might in a way that multiplies
our own efforts many times over.
SHIRLEY DOBSON

As you pray, ask God to give you that day
a single mind, a submissive mind,
a spiritual mind, and a secure mind.
WARREN WIERSBE

> You pay God a compliment
> by asking great things of Him.
>
> ST. TERESA OF AVILA

> When you ask God to do something,
> don't ask timidly;
> put your whole heart into it.
>
> MARIE T. FREEMAN

> I have found the perfect antidote for fear.
> Whenever it sticks up its ugly face,
> I clobber it with prayer.
>
> DALE EVANS

THANK YOU FOR . . . YOUR PRAYERS

PRAYER SUCCEEDS WHEN ALL ELSE FAILS.

E. M. BOUNDS

> I'M A HUNDRED AND TWO YEARS OLD, AND I STILL PRAY FOR MY CHILDREN EVERY DAY. I ALWAYS HAVE; I ALWAYS WILL.
>
> — MARIE T. FREEMAN

Thank You for...
THE LESSONS

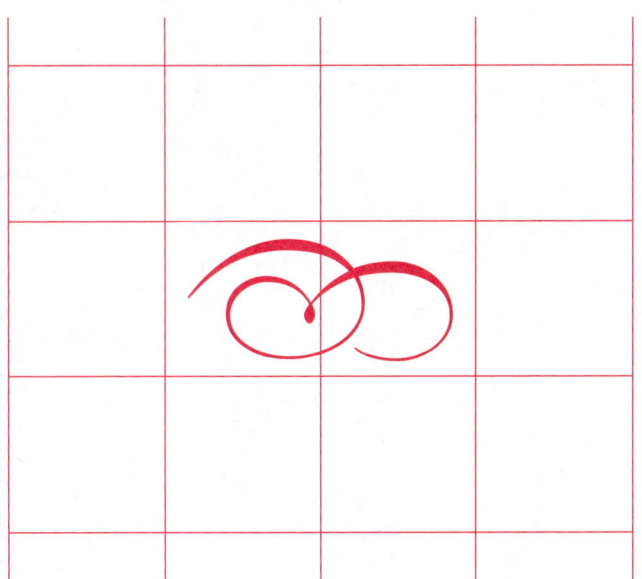

*Train up a child in the way he should go,
and when he is old he will not depart from it.*

PROVERBS 22:6 NKJV

DEAR MOM,

Mothers not only give life, they teach it. That's exactly what you've done. For longer than I can remember, you've taught me life's most important lessons. You are the teacher, I am the pupil, and class is still in session.

One of life's great ironies is that there is so much to learn and so little time. I value the lessons you have taught me *and* the ones I still have to learn.

THANK YOU FOR . . . THE LESSONS

> LESSONS LEARNED
> AT MOTHER'S KNEE
> LAST THROUGH LIFE.
>
> LAURA INGALLS WILDER

Most mothers are instinctive philosophers.
HARRIET BEECHER STOWE

The best academy is a mother's knee.
JAMES RUSSELL LOWELL

The art of teaching is
the art of assisting discovery.
MARK VAN DOREN

THE MOTHER IS AND MUST BE, WHETHER SHE KNOWS IT OR NOT, THE GREATEST, STRONGEST, AND MOST LASTING TEACHER HER CHILDREN HAVE.

HANNAH WHITALL SMITH

> There is so much to teach,
> and the time goes so fast.
>
> ERMA BOMBECK

> A mother is not a person to lean on,
> but a person to make leaning unnecessary.
>
> DOROTHY CANFIELD FISHER

> In the final analysis it is not what you do
> for your children but what you have taught
> them to do for themselves that will make them
> successful human beings.
>
> ANN LANDERS

THANK YOU FOR . . . THE LESSONS

> THE MOTHER'S HEART IS THE CHILD'S SCHOOLROOM.

HENRY WARD BEECHER

THANK YOU FOR BEING MY MOTHER

My mother taught me everything.
Everything.

BARBARA EDEN

A child will hear his mother's voice
for the rest of his life.

TERRY SAVAGE

I do not teach children, I give them joy.

ISADORA DUNCAN

THANK YOU FOR... THE LESSONS

Better to instruct a child than to collect riches.

HERVE OF BRITTANY

While we teach, we learn.

SENECA

Children have more need of models than critics.

JOSEPH JOUBERT

Raising children requires courage,
not to mention a sense of humor.

LIZ CURTIS HIGGS

> A home is a place where we find direction.
>
> GIGI GRAHAM TCHIVIDJIAN

> If your experiences would benefit anybody, give them to someone.
>
> FLORENCE NIGHTINGALE

> Train your child in the way in which you know you should have gone yourself.
>
> C. H. SPURGEON

Thank You for...
YOUR SACRIFICES

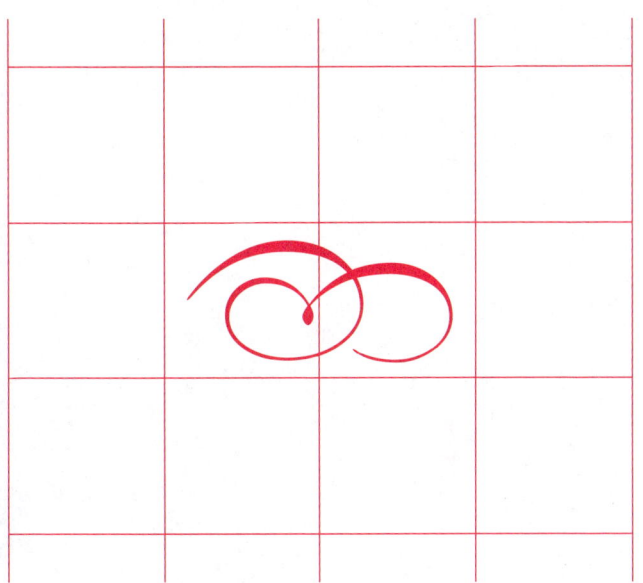

The generous soul will be made rich.

PROVERBS 11:25 NKJV

DEAR MOM,

Thank you for the countless sacrifices you've made. A caring mother gives everything to her family, and that's exactly what you've done for us. Along the way, you've earned our devotion, our respect, our care, and our love.

Raising a family requires an endless supply of love, patience, understanding, and work. But throughout all the busy days and all the sleepless nights, you have remained steadfast.

Motherhood is more art than science, more guesswork than certainty. But one thing remains sure: You've never stopped giving, and we've never stopped noticing.

A family is one of nature's masterpieces.
GEORGE SANTAYANA

Family is the we of me.
CARSON MCCULLERS

A family is the first and essential cell of human society.
POPE JOHN XXIII

THANK YOU FOR BEING MY MOTHER

The family—that dear octopus from whose
tentacles we never quite escape, nor,
in our inmost hearts, ever quite wish to.

DODIE SMITH

To talk about parenting without involvement
is like talking about a business venture
without investment.

GILBERT BEERS

Family life! The United Nations is child's play
compared to the tugs and splits and need
to understand and forgive in any family.

MAY SARTON

THANK YOU FOR... YOUR SACRIFICES

> The best gift parents can give children is themselves.
>
> ANONYMOUS

> Call it a clan, call it a network, call it a tribe, call it a family. Whatever you call it, whoever you are, you need one.
>
> JANE HOWARD

> No kingdom divided can stand—neither can a household.
>
> CHRISTINE DE PISAN

THANK YOU FOR BEING MY MOTHER

A family is a school of duties...founded on love.
FELIX ADLER

Children are the hands by which
we take hold of heaven.
HENRY WARD BEECHER

A happy family is but an earlier heaven.
SIR JOHN BOWRING

A large family gives beauty to a house.
INDIAN PROVERB

THANK YOU FOR . . . YOUR SACRIFICES

A family divided against itself
will perish together.
INDIAN PROVERB

When the whole family is together,
the soul is in place.
RUSSIAN PROVERB

Cherish your human connections:
your relationships with friends and family.
BARBARA BUSH

You leave home to seek your fortune,
and when you get it, you go home
and share it with your family.
ANITA BAKER

> Healthy families are our greatest national resource.
>
> DOLORES CURRAN

> The family is the nucleus of civilization.
>
> WILL AND ARIEL DURANT

> Our children are not going to be just "our children" they are going to be other people's husbands and wives and the parents of our grandchildren.
>
> MARY STEICHEN CALDERONE

THANK YOU FOR . . . YOUR SACRIFICES

> YOU DON'T CHOOSE
> YOUR FAMILY.
> THEY ARE GOD'S GIFT
> TO YOU, AS YOU ARE
> TO THEM.
>
> DESMOND TUTU

THANK YOU FOR BEING MY MOTHER

What families have in common the world around is that they are the place where people learn who they are and how to be that way.

JEAN ILLSLEY CLARKE

The debt of gratitude we owe our mother and father goes forward, not backward. What we owe our parents is the bill presented to us by our children.

NANCY FRIDAY

Home, in one form or another, is the great objective of life.

JOSIAH GILBERT HOLLAND

The happiest moments of my life have been spent in the bosom of my family.

THOMAS JEFFERSON

THANK YOU FOR . . . YOUR SACRIFICES

THE WOMAN IS THE HEART OF THE HOME.

MOTHER TERESA

THANK YOU FOR BEING MY MOTHER

IT TAKES A HEAP OF LIVIN' IN A HOUSE TO MAKE IT HOME.

EDGAR A. GUEST

Thank You for...

YOUR EXAMPLE

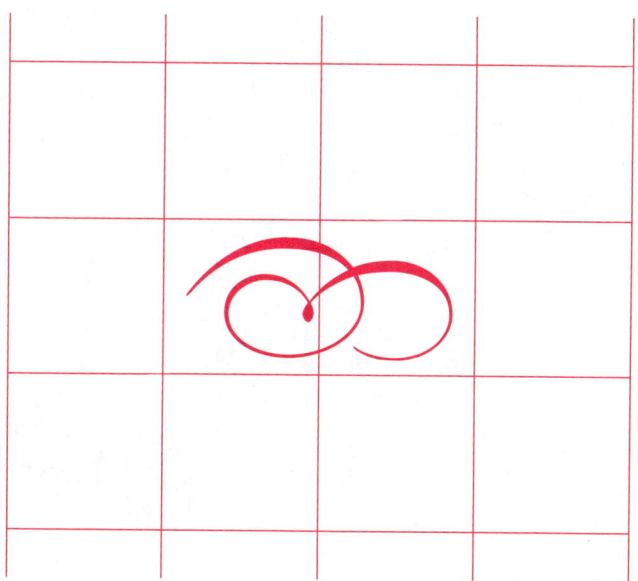

*Be an example to the believers in word,
in conduct, in love, in spirit, in faith, in purity.*

1 TIMOTHY 4:12 NKJV

DEAR MOM,

Thanks for the example you've set. You have taught me some of life's most important lessons, not only by your words but also by your actions. You weren't always perfect—nobody is—but when you made mistakes, you corrected them, and moved on.

I have been blessed by your example. I'll happily spend the rest of my life trying, as best I can, to live up to the standards you have set.

THANK YOU FOR . . . YOUR EXAMPLE

> THERE IS
> A TRANSCENDENT POWER
> IN EXAMPLE.
> WE REFORM OTHERS
> UNCONSCIOUSLY WHEN
> WE WALK UPRIGHTLY.

ANNE SOPHIE SWETCHINE

THE POWER OF EXAMPLE
IN A PARENT DOES MORE
TO TRAIN A CHILD
THAN ANY OTHER
SINGLE THING.

LARRY CHRISTENSON

THANK YOU FOR... YOUR EXAMPLE

Let us preach you, Dear Jesus,
without preaching, not by words but by
our example, by the casting force,
the sympathetic influence of what we do,
the evident fullness of the love
our hearts bear to you. Amen.

MOTHER TERESA

An ounce of loving role modeling is worth
a pound of parental pressure.

GILBERT BEERS

There can be no happiness if the things we
believe in are different from the things we do.

FREYA STARK

A person's action is only a picture book
of his creed.

RALPH WALDO EMERSON

If a child sees his parents day in and day out
behaving with self-discipline, restraint,
dignity, and a capacity to order their lives,
then the child will come to feel in
the deepest fibers of his being that
this is the way to live.

M. SCOTT PECK

THANK YOU FOR . . . YOUR EXAMPLE

IF YOU WANT YOUR CHILD
TO ACCEPT YOUR VALUES,
THEN YOU MUST
BE WORTHY OF
HIS RESPECT.

JAMES DOBSON

A person who lives right and is right
has more power in his silence
han another has by words.

PHILLIPS BROOKS

Actions speak louder than words;
let your words teach and your actions speak.

ST. ANTHONY OF PADUA

Our children do not follow our words
but our actions.

JAMES BALDWIN

THANK YOU FOR . . . YOUR EXAMPLE

> DON'T WORRY THAT YOUR CHILDREN NEVER LISTEN TO YOU; WORRY THAT THEY ARE ALWAYS WATCHING YOU.
>
> ROBERT FULGHUM

THANK YOU FOR BEING MY MOTHER

YOUR DAILY LIFE IS YOUR TEMPLE AND YOUR RELIGION.

KHALIL GIBRAN

THANK YOU FOR... YOUR EXAMPLE

Not only should we teach values,
but we should live them. My kids pay
a lot more attention to what I do than
what I say. A sermon is better lived
than preached.

J. C. WATTS

Our walk counts far more than our talk, always!

GEORGE MUELLER

> IF YOU WANT TO BE RESPECTED FOR YOUR ACTIONS, THEN YOUR BEHAVIOR MUST BE ABOVE REPROACH.
>
> ROSA PARKS

> THANK YOU FOR . . . YOUR EXAMPLE

WE TEACH WHO WE ARE.

JOHN GARDNER

THANK YOU FOR BEING MY MOTHER

MY LIFE IS MY MESSAGE.

GANDHI

A Mother Is...

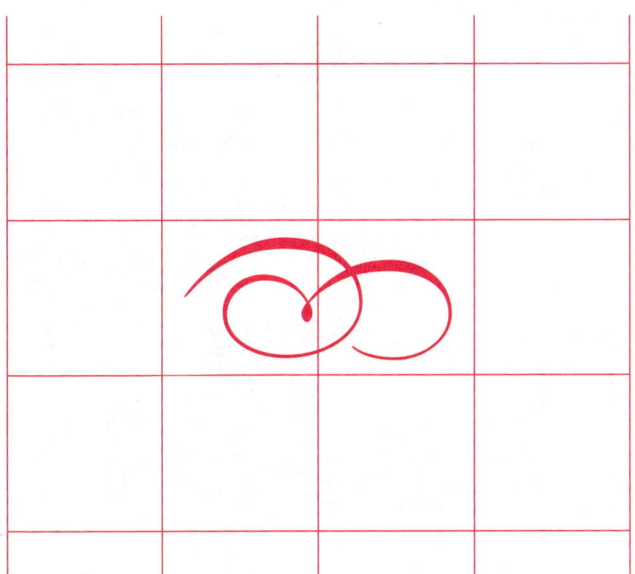

*Honor your father and your mother,
that your days may be long upon the land
which the Lord your God is giving you.*

EXODUS 20:12 NKJV

DEAR MOM,

A mother is many things: She is the giver of life and love, the maker of house and home. She is chief cook and bottle washer, babysitter of last resort, provider, educator, doctor, disciplinarian, spiritual guide, counselor, health inspector, clothing consultant, and taxi driver.

Being a mother can be a complicated, exhausting job. But even when times have been tough, you've succeeded. May God bless you always!

A MOTHER IS . . .

MOTHERHOOD IS
THE GREATEST PRIVILEGE
OF LIFE.

MARY ROPER COKER

The role of mother is probably
the most important career a woman can have.

JANET MARY RILEY

Every mother is like Moses.
She does not enter the promised land.
She prepares a world she will not see.

POPE PAUL VI

A MOTHER IS . . .

Being a full-time mom is the hardest job
I've ever had, but it is also the best job
I've ever had. The pay is lousy,
but the rewards are eternal.

LISA WHELCHEL

The mother is the unchartered servant
of the future.

KATHERINE ANTHONY

BEING A MOTHER,
AS FAR AS I CAN TELL,
IS A CONSTANTLY
EVOLVING PROCESS OF
ADAPTING TO THE NEEDS
OF YOUR CHILD WHILE
ALSO CHANGING
AND GROWING AS
A PERSON IN YOUR
OWN RIGHT.

DEBORAH INSEL

A MOTHER IS . . .

MOTHERHOOD IS THE BIGGEST ON-THE-JOB TRAINING PROGRAM IN EXISTENCE TODAY.

ERMA BOMBECK

THANK YOU FOR BEING MY MOTHER

BEING A MOTHER ISN'T MY JOB; IT'S MY LIFE.

MARIE T. FREEMAN

ABOUT CRISWELL FREEMAN

Criswell Freeman's books have sold millions of copies, yet his name is largely unknown to the general public. *The Wall Street Journal* observed, "Normally, a tally like that would put a writer on the bestseller lists. But Freeman is hardly a household name." And that's exactly how the author likes it.

The Washington Post called Freeman "possibly the most prolific 'quote book' writer in America." With little fanfare, Dr. Freeman has compiled and edited well over a hundred titles that have now sold over 8,000,000 copies.

Freeman began his writing career as a self-help author (his first book was entitled *When Life Throws You a Curveball, Hit It)*. Today, Freeman's writings focus on the Good News of God's Holy Word. Criswell is a Doctor of Clinical Psychology (he earned his degree from the Adler School of Professional Psychology in Chicago). He earned his undergraduate degree at Vanderbilt University. Freeman also attended classes at The Southern Baptist Theological Seminary in Louisville where he studied under the noted pastoral counselor Wayne Oates.

Criswell lives in Nashville, Tennessee. He is married and has two daughters.